PROMOTION PROTOCOL™

COACHING CONVERSATIONS

Companion Guide

Kim Nugent, Ed.D.

Promotion Protocol™: Coaching Conversations.
Companion Guide
Copyright © 2018 by Dr. Kim Nugent. All rights reserved

Publisher: Sojourn Publishing
ISBN: 978-1-62747-282-1

Contact Dr. Kim Nugent at:
Email: Kim@PromotionProtocol.com
Web: PromotionProtocol.com | DrNugentSpeaks.com

Credits:
Cover Designers: Gagan Sarkaria, M.F.A, M.B.A, & Abbey Wilkerson, B.F.A. UnfoldYourSuccess.com
Interior Layout & Design: Gagan Sarkaria & Abbey Wilkerson
Book Cover Sales Copy & Content Editing: Gagan Sarkaria
Author Photo: Lisa Crosby

Promotion Protocol Complete Branding, Art Direction, Design
& Production: Gagan Sarkaria & Abbey Wilkerson
Presentation / Slide Deck Designer: Gagan Sarkaria
eBooks: Gagan Sarkaria & Abbey Wilkerson

PROMOTION PROTOCOL™

COACHING CONVERSATIONS

Companion Guide

Kim Nugent, Ed.D.

Kim Nugent, Ed.D.

Mentoring A New Generation of Exceptional Leaders

www.PromotionProtocol.com

Kim Nugent is an innovation leadership coach with an exceptional track record across generations of mentoring aspiring leaders into exceptional leadership positions. In addition, Kim is a best-selling author of the books: *Did I Say Never?* and *52 Weeks to Exceptional Leadership*.

Kim believes if you want to achieve extraordinary results, you must start with your people. Investing time, training, and mentoring to bring out the best in each individual is the first step in the process. The next step is to build a culture of sustainability through a customized mentoring system to achieve key performance indicators. If you would like to find out how, contact Kim at: Kim@PromotionProtocol.com.

THIS BOOK BELONGS TO:

Phone:

Email:

SELF-ASSESSMENT INVENTORY INSTRUCTIONS

What if we created a win-win situation? Let's begin by starting the self-assessment inventory. Please take it before you apply for the next promotion; self-assess. **Let's get started.**

If you are the *employee* and are reading this to improve your chances of getting promoted, please begin by completing the self-assessment. In the first column, rate yourself in each category from 1 to 10; 1 being poor and 10 being excellent. Do not skip any of the twenty-six categories. Save the second column for your weekly coaching meetings.

If you are the *supervisor*, schedule weekly coaching meetings. Read through the questions before you meet with the employee, so you have a sense of where you want to take the conversation. Feel free to enhance the questions based on your company's culture and environment. This approach will help you mentor a new generation of aspiring leaders. Know that by using this approach you are leaving a legacy for our high-potentials to step into their future.

Self-Assessment Inventory

ABC's of Promotability	Plan to Improve/Resources Utilized
Rate Yourself 1-10. 1 Being Poor, 10 Being Excellent.	
1 2 3 4 5 6 7 8 9 10 Attitude	
1 2 3 4 5 6 7 8 9 10 Brand	
1 2 3 4 5 6 7 8 9 10 Communication	
1 2 3 4 5 6 7 8 9 10 Depth	
1 2 3 4 5 6 7 8 9 10 Energy	
1 2 3 4 5 6 7 8 9 10 Focus	
1 2 3 4 5 6 7 8 9 10 Gratitude	

ABC's of Promotability	Plan to Improve/Resources Utilized
Rate Yourself 1-10. 1 Being Poor, 10 Being Excellent.	

1	2	3	4	5	6	7	8	9	10

Habits

1	2	3	4	5	6	7	8	9	10

Integrity

1	2	3	4	5	6	7	8	9	10

Jaded

1	2	3	4	5	6	7	8	9	10

Knowledgeable

1	2	3	4	5	6	7	8	9	10

Life-Long Learner

1	2	3	4	5	6	7	8	9	10

Mindset

1	2	3	4	5	6	7	8	9	10

Network

1	2	3	4	5	6	7	8	9	10

Opportunity

1	2	3	4	5	6	7	8	9	10

Problem-Solver

1	2	3	4	5	6	7	8	9	10

Question

ABC's of Promotability	Plan to Improve/Resources Utilized

Rate Yourself 1-10. 1 Being Poor, 10 Being Excellent.

1	2	3	4	5	6	7	8	9	10

Responsibility

1	2	3	4	5	6	7	8	9	10

Self-Awareness

1	2	3	4	5	6	7	8	9	10

Thank You

1	2	3	4	5	6	7	8	9	10

Unique

1	2	3	4	5	6	7	8	9	10

Vision

1	2	3	4	5	6	7	8	9	10

White Lies

1	2	3	4	5	6	7	8	9	10

X-Factor

1	2	3	4	5	6	7	8	9	10

Yearning

1	2	3	4	5	6	7	8	9	10

Zone

A

ATTITUDE

" A positive attitude gives you power over your circumstances instead of allowing your circumstances to have power over you.

— Joyce Meyer

Self-Assessment Questions

Question:

How self-aware are you?

Response:

Question:

Have you ever taken an attitude assessment? Have you ever had a 360-degree performance assessment in your career? If yes, what did it reveal?

Response:

Question:

If you were to ask your peers about your attitude, what would they say? Interview 3 to 5 people you trust that will give you direct feedback about your attitude.

Response:

Question:

What would your supervisor say regarding your attitude? If you do not know, ask.

Response:

Question:

If you have direct reports, what would they say?

Response:

Question:

What would your family say about your attitude?

Response:

Question:

When you hit a roadblock at work, how do you handle it?

Response:

Question:

Do you feel like you are resilient? If yes, give an example.

Response:

Question:

In what area do you think you excel?

Response:

Question:

What is one area in which you could improve your attitude?

Response:

Question:

What is one action step you can take to improve in this area?

Response:

Question:

How will you know you are making progress?

Response:

Coach/Mentor Questions

Q: Describe your attitude self-assessment.

Response:

Q: Did you ask others for feedback about your attitude?

Response:

Q: Did you learn anything new?

Response:

Q: Did any comments surprise you?

Response:

Q: What is one action step you can take to improve your attitude?

Response:

Q: How will you measure your improvement in this area?

Response:

Q: How can I support you?

Response:

B

BRAND

"Your brand is what people say about you when you are not in the room.

— Jeff Bezos, Amazon

Self-Assessment Questions

Question:

What does your brand communicate about you?

Response:

Question:

What would people say about you, if you were not in the room? If you do not know, find out.

Response:

Question:

How self-aware are you? 1 being poor and 10 being excellent

Response:

Question:

On a scale of 1-10, how strong is your brand?
   a. Face-to-face
   b. Communication
   c. Social Media accounts

Response:

Question:

What is one area in which you could improve your brand at work?

Response:

Question:

Have you set up a LinkedIn profile? How can it be improved?

Response:

Question:

What is one area in which you could improve your brand on your social-media accounts? Is there anything you have posted in the past that might have you concerned?

Response:

Question:

How will you learn more about developing your personal brand?

Response:

Question:

What is one action step you can take to improve your brand?

Response:

Question:

How will you know you are making progress?

Response:

Coach/Mentor Questions

Q: Describe your brand's self-assessment.

Response:

Q: What did you learn from the Fast Company article on "Brand Your Survival Kit" by Tom Peters?

Response:

Q: Did you ask others for feedback at work?

Response:

Q: Did you ask others for feedback on your social-media accounts?

Response:

Q: Did you learn anything new?

Response:

Q: Did any comments surprise you?

Response:

Q: What is one action you can take to improve in this area?

Response:

Q: How will you measure your improvement in this area?

Response:

Q: How can I support you?

Response:

C

COMMUNICATION

" The art of communication is the language of leadership.

— James Humes

Self-Assessment Questions

Rate your communication skills on a scale of 1-10 with 1 being poor and 10 being excellent.

Response:

_____ Listening

_____ Speaking

_____ Writing

_____ Presenting

_____ Facilitating

_____ Nonverbal Communication

_____ Body Language

_____ Tone of Voice

Question:

What is an area you need to start on first?

Response:

Question:

What is one area you could improve your communication skills at work?

Response:

Question:

What outside resources will help you improve in this area?

Response:

Question:

Have you ever participated in Toastmasters, Dale Carnegie, National Speakers Association or personal-development courses to improve your communication?

Response:

Question:

How will you know you are making progress?

Response:

Coach/Mentor Questions

Q: Describe your communication skill strengths.

Response:

Q: Describe your communication skill weaknesses.

Response:

Q: How important do you think effective communication skills are for our organization?

Response:

Q: Have you ever participated in Toastmasters, Dale Carnegie, National Speakers Association or personal-development courses to improve your communication?

Response:

Q: Are you open to joining a local Toastmasters group?

Response:

Q: What is one action you can take to improve in this area?

Response:

Q: How will you measure your improvement in this area?

Response:

Q: How can I support you?

Response:

D

DEPTH

"To nurture the sort of relationships that will surely help propel you towards accomplishing great things, you need to forget transactional networking and focus on having in-depth conversations with fewer people about subjects you really care about.

— Naveen Jain

Self-Assessment Questions

Question:

In what areas do you need to expand your personal depth?

Response:

Question:

What is an area of interest that you want to explore or deepen first?

Response:

Question:

What is one area where you could improve your creativity, or right brain?

Response:

Question:

What is one area you could improve your business knowledge, or left brain at work?

Response:

Coach/Mentor Questions

Q: Describe how you have developed your personal depth and interests at this point in yourself.

Response:

Q: What area are you excited about expanding?

Response:

Q: What area are you nervous about expanding?

Response:

Q: What area in your life have you noticed you say "no" to instead of "yes"?

Response:

Q: Where have you said "no" in your life that you might be open to answering "yes" now?

Response:

Q: Tell me more about the reason you have not tried it or what you tell yourself you cannot do?

Response:

Q: How will you measure your improvement in this area?

Response:

Q: How can I support you?

Response:

E

ENERGY

"And what is a man without energy? Nothing – nothing at all.
— Mark Twain

Self-Assessment Questions

Question:

On a scale of 1-10 with 1 being poor and 10 being excellent, how would you rate your energy level?

Response:

Question:

What personal energy areas could be improved upon?

Response:

_____ Healthy eating

_____ Exercise daily

_____ Drinking more water

_____ Sleeping at least 8 hours a night

_____ Relationships

_____ Setting goals

Question:

What is an area of interest to start on first?

Response:

Question:

What actions will you take?

Response:

Question:

How will you know you are making progress?

Response:

Coach/Mentor Questions

Q: Describe your personal energy level at this point in your life.

Response:

Q: How can you improve your energy level based on your personal assessment?

Response:

Q: With what area will you start?

Response:

—— Healthy eating

—— Exercise daily

—— Drinking more water

—— Sleeping at least 8 hours a night

—— Relationships

—— Setting goals

Q: Do you feel you surround yourself with positive people who add to your life? If there is anyone who might be toxic for you, what will you do about it?

Response:

Q: What are you passionate about? What goals have you set for yourself?

Response:

Q: What do you want your life to stand for?

Response:

Q: What do you want in your life?

Response:

Q: How will you measure your improvement in this area?

Response:

Q: How can I support you?

Response:

F

FOCUS

" You can do anything as long as
you have the passion, the drive,
the focus, and the support.

— Sabrina Bryan

Self-Assessment Questions

Question:

Is being focused a strength or a challenge for you?

Response:

Question:

In what areas are you distracted?

Response:

Question:

Do you think you are an adrenalin junkie?

Response:

Question:

How can you mitigate these distractions from happening? Addicted to the stress?

Response:

Question:

What is one action step you can put in place today?

Response:

Question:

How will you know you are making progress?

Response:

Coach/Mentor Questions

Q: How do you stay focused for the day?

Response:

Q: How do you stay focused for the day?

Response:

Q: What are areas of distraction for you?

Response:

Q: How can you mitigate these?

Response:

Q: How will you measure your improvement in this area?

Response:

Q: How can I support you?

Response:

GRATITUDE

"
Gratitude makes sense of our past, brings peace for today, and creates a vision for tomorrow.

— Melody Beattie

Self-Assessment Questions

Question:

Do you keep a gratitude journal?

Response:

Question:

Would you be willing to write out what you are grateful for each morning?

Response:

Question:

How do you think it might change your perspective?

Response:

Question:

In what areas of your life have you taken people or situations for granted?

Response:

Question:

What is one action step you can put into place today regarding gratitude?

Response:

How will you know you are making progress?

Response:

Coach/Mentor Questions

Q: What are you grateful for at work?

Response:

Q: What are you grateful for at home?

Response:

Q: What are you grateful for from your work team?

Response:

Q: What are you grateful for in your relationships?

Response:

Q: What daily practice are you willing to take to keep gratitude at the forefront?

Response:

Q: Is there any area of your life or a person you have taken for granted?

Response:

Q: How will you measure your improvement in this area?

Response:

Q: How can I support you?

Response:

HABITS

> " We are what we repeatedly do.
> Excellence then is not an act
> but a habit.
>
> — Aristotle

Self-Assessment Questions

Question:

What habits need to change?

Response:

Question:

What is the habit you are going to work on first?

Response:

Question:

What is the underlying cause of the poor habits?

Response:

Question:

Are you willing to have an accountability partner? If so, who could be your partner?

Response:

Question:

What is the time-frame you are committing to change the habit?

Response:

Question:

How will you know you are making progress?

Response:

Question:

How will you celebrate your success?

Response:

Coach/Mentor Questions

Q: What habit have you decided to work on first?

Response:

Q: How will it lead to excellence?

Response:

Q: What is the benefit to making this change?

Response:

Q: What will it cost you if you do not make the change?

Response:

Q: How will you feel when you change this habit?

Response:

Q: Do you have an accountability partner?

Response:

Q: How will you keep this present and at the top of your mind daily?

Response:

Q: What is your time-frame?

Response:

Q: If you make a misstep, how will you recover and get back on track?

Response:

Q: How will you measure your improvement in this area?

Response:

Q: How will we celebrate your success?

Response:

Q: How can I support you?

Response:

I

INTEGRITY

" A single lie destroys a whole reputation of integrity.

— Baltasar Gracian

Self-Assessment Questions

Question:

What does integrity mean to you?

Response:

Question:

Is integrity important in a leadership role?

Response:

Question:

When you read the examples, did you see yourself in any of them?

Response:

Question:

Who do you admire because of their integrity? What company displays integrity?

Response:

Question:

What examples are you aware of in business when the leader failed to have integrity? What happened? If not aware, research and share.

Response:

Question:

What is one area that you can work on for yourself?

Response:

Question:

How do you justify your behavior when your integrity is not intact?

Response:

Question:

How will you know you are making progress?

Response:

Question:

How will you know when you can keep your word? To yourself? To others?

Response:

Coach/Mentor Questions

Q: What does integrity mean to you?

Response:

Q: What did you think of some of the examples provided? Let's discuss a few.

Response:

Q: Have you ever looked at integrity in this way? What surprised you?

Response:

Q: If you were in a leadership position, how would you model it?

Response:

Q: In your current position, how do you demonstrate integrity?

Response:

Q: What happens when a leader does not model integrity? What happens to the organization? To the culture? To the people? Can you give me some specific examples?

Response:

How will you measure your improvement in this area?

Response:

How can I support you?

Response:

J

JADED

"I suppose there are a lot of reasons to be jaded or sarcastic, but I hang onto the reasons why life is beautiful.

— Kellie O'Hara

Self-Assessment Questions

Question:

On a scale of 1 to 10 with 1 - being feel jaded all the time and 10 being never feel jaded. How would you rate yourself?

Response:

Question:

In what areas do you struggle with cynicism?

Response:

Question:

How can you begin to change this outlook?

Response:

Question:

How will you know you are starting to shift your perspective?

Response:

Coach/Mentor Questions

Q: Are there areas at work where you feel jaded? What happened?

Response:

Q: What is the root cause?

Response:

Q: How can you change your perspective?

Response:

Q: If you have a direct report who is jaded, how would you coach that employee? How can you propose an alternative perspective?

Response:

Q: What strategies might work to improve the situation?

Response:

Q: What resources might be available?

Response:

Q: How can I support your growth in this area?

Response:

K

KNOWLEDGEABLE

" An investment in knowledge
pays the best interest.
— Benjamin Franklin

Self-Assessment Questions

On a scale of 1 to 10, with 1 - poorly and 10 - very well how well do you understand the following?

Response:

_____ Company culture

_____ Company mission, vision, and values

_____ Company strategic plan

_____ Company policies and procedures

_____ Company metrics

_____ Company reports

_____ Your role with this company

_____ Overall company operations

_____ Finances/Budget

_____ Technology

_____ Talent development

_____ Promotion protocol

Question:

Once you have completed the list, decide where to start. What is the first action step to increase your knowledge?

Response:

Question:

What is your plan to gain more knowledge about the company? Write out the plan and be ready to share with your coach/supervisor. This is a crucial conversation.

Response:

Question:

What way do you learn best?

Response:

_____ Auditory

_____ Visual

_____ Tactile-Kinesthetic

_____ Online

_____ Face-to-face

_____ Blended

_____ Research on own

_____ Books

_____ Podcasts

_____ Workshops

_____ College classes

Question:

What resources are available within the company to acquire new knowledge?

Response:

Question:

How can you become a highly valued contributor?

Response:

Coach/Mentor Questions

Q: In what areas do you feel you need to gain more knowledge about company operations? Share with me your plan and list of things you need to learn so we can incorporate those into our weekly meetings.

Response:

_____ Company culture

_____ Company mission, vision, and values

_____ Company strategic plan

_____ Company policies and procedures

_____ Company metrics

_____ Company reports

_____ Your role with this company

_____ Overall company operations

_____ Finances/Budget

_____ Technology

_____ Talent development

_____ Promotion protocol

Q: Where do you want to start? Let's create a plan.

Response:

Q: Do you have a mentor?

Response:

Q: How do you learn best?

Response:

———— Auditory

———— Visual

———— Tactile-Kinesthetic

———— Online

———— Face-to-face

———— Blended

———— Research on own

———— Books

———— Podcasts

———— Workshops

———— College classes

Q: How do you want to be coached?

Response:

Q: What resources do you think you need?

Response:

Q: How can I support your growth in this area?

Response:

LIFE-LONG LEARNER

"Life is not about finding
yourself. Life is about
creating it.

— George Bernard Shaw

Self-Assessment Questions

Question:

On a scale of 1 to 10 rate yourself with 1 - being I do not care to learn and 10 - I have a passion for learning.

Response:

_____ Love of learning

Question:

What types of topics interest you?

Response:

Question:

What was the last personal-development course you took?

Response:

Question:

Have you watched TedTalks on YouTube? What are three of your favorites?

Response:

Question:

What was the last book you read or listened to?

Response:

Question:

What podcasts do you listen to?

Response:

Question:

Do you speak more than one language?

Response:

Question:

What have you done to develop your creativity?

Response:

Question:

What interests you?

Response:

Question:

Where can lessons be learned from other industries?

Response:

Question:

What customer-service examples can you provide?

Response:

How can you encourage others to be life-long learners?

Coach/Mentor Questions

Q: How did you rate yourself on the topic of being a life-long learner? Explain.

Response:

Q: What areas of learning do you enjoy?

Response:

Q: What was the last personal development course you took?

Response:

Q: What was the last book you read or listened to?

Response:

Q: Do you watch TedTalks? If yes, what is one of your favorites?

Response:

Q: What podcasts do you listen to?

Response:

Q: Do you speak more than one language?

Response:

Q: What have you done to develop your creativity?

Response:

Q: What areas do you find less appealing?

Response:

Q: How can you encourage others to be life-long learners?

Response:

Q: Give me two examples of excellent customer service you have noticed.

Response:

Q: Give me one example of poor customer service you received.

Response:

Q: How can we share opportunities for growth in this area?

Response:

MINDSET

Self-Assessment Questions

Question:

Overall, do you feel like you have a growth mindset or a fixed mindset?

Response:

Question:

In what areas of your life, do you have a growth mindset?

Response:

Question:

In what areas of your life do you have a fixed mindset?

Response:

Question:

Do you like to be rewarded for the outcome or the journey?

Response:

Question:

What do you say to yourself when things are hard, or you are learning something for the very first time?

Response:

Question:

How can you begin to shift your mindset to a growth mindset?

Response:

Question:

How will you know you are starting to shift your perspective?

Response:

Coach/Mentor Questions

Q: Describe what you think is a growth mindset.

Response:

Q: Describe what you think is a fixed mindset.

Response:

Q: Do you feel like you have a growth mindset or fixed mindset?

Response:

Q: In what areas of your life, do you have a growth mindset?

Response:

Q: In what areas of your life do you have a fixed mindset?

Response:

Q: Do you like to be rewarded for the outcome or the journey? Explain.

Response:

Q: What do you say to yourself when things are hard, or you are learning something for the very first time?

Response:

Q: How can you begin to shift your mindset of a growth mindset?

Response:

Q: How will you know you are starting to shift your perspective?

Response:

Q: How can I encourage your growth in this area?

Response:

Q: We are halfway through the 26 traits, what you do feel you have learned to date?

Response:

Q: How do you feel you have changed?

Response:

NETWORK

"One of the most powerful networking practices is to provide immediate value to a new connection. This means the moment you identify a way to help someone you take action.

— Lewis Howes

Self-Assessment Questions

Question:

What is the purpose of networking?

Response:

Question:

How can it help your career?

Response:

Question:

Do you enjoy networking?

Response:

Question:

In what areas of networking do you feel you need assistance?

Response:

Question:

In what areas of networking do you excel?

Response:

Question:

What was the last networking event you attended?

Response:

Question:

When and where is the next networking event you will attend?

Response:

Question:

What value can you create when networking?

Response:

Coach/Mentor Questions

Q: What networking events have you attended within our company and externally?

Response:

Q: Describe how you feel when you go to a networking event?

Response:

Q: Do you typically go alone to these events or do you bring another colleague with you?

Response:

Q: In what areas of networking do you feel you excel?

Response:

Q: In what areas of networking do you need assistance with now?

Response:

Q: Is there a networking event that you are interested in attending but have not done so yet?

Response:

Q: What is stopping you?you?

Response:

Q: How can I support your growth in this area?

Response:

OPPORTUNITY

" Success is where preparation
and opportunity meet.

— Bobby Unser

Self-Assessment Questions

Question:

What problems or gaps have you noticed in the organization that could be viewed as opportunities?

Response:

Question:

When have you taken the initiative to bring solutions to your organization? Provide three examples.

Response:

1.

2.

3.

Question:

What kind of impact do you want to make?

Response:

Question:

How will you know you are making progress?

Response:

Coach/Mentor Questions

Q: Did you learn anything new when you read the example shared as an opportunity?

Response:

Q: What problems or gaps have you noticed in the organization that could be viewed as opportunities?

Response:

Q: When have you taken the initiative to bring solutions to your organization? Provide three examples.

Response:

1.

2.

3.

Q: What kind of impact do you want to make?

Response:

Q: What is one action you can take to improve in this area?

Response:

Q: How will you measure your improvement in this area?

Response:

Q: How can I support you?

Response:

P

PROBLEM-SOLVER

" Never bring the problem-solving stage into the decision-making stage. Otherwise, you surrender yourself to the problem rather than the solution.

— Robert Schuller

Self-Assessment Questions

Question:

When problems are presented, how do you begin to solve them?

Response:

Question:

Research 3 problem-solving models to help you become a better problem-solver.

Response:

1.

2.

3.

Question:

What problems have you solved at work? Provide three examples.

Response:

1.

2.

3.

Question:

How will you know you are making progress in the area of problem-solving?

Response:

Coach/Mentor Questions

Q: When problems are presented, how do you begin to solve them?

Response:

Q: Research 3 problem-solving models to help you become a better problem-solver. Be ready to discuss the pros and cons of each approach.

Response:

1.

2.

3.

Q: What problems have you solved at work? Provide three examples.

Response:

1.

2.

3.

Q: When you begin to solve a problem, do you look at the root cause?

Response:

Q: How do you identify the issue? How do you determine the solution(s)?

Response:

Q: How can you help your team members become better problem-solvers?

Response:

Q: How will you know you are making progress in the area of problem-solving?

Response:

Q: How can I support you?

Response:

QUESTION

" The art and science of asking questions is the source of all knowledge.

— Thomas Berger

Self-Assessment Questions

Question:

How is problem-solving related to asking questions?

Response:

Question:

Have you ever thought about the types of questions you ask?

Response:

Question:

Does your organization have a questioning model they use?

Response:

Question:

Research 3 questioning resources. It can be online, book, podcast or TedTalk.
Be ready to discuss.

Response:

1.

2.

3.

Question:

How will you know you are improving your questioning ability?

Response:

Coach/Mentor Questions

Q: It seems that problem-solving and asking questions are related. Explain to me the relationship and how it can enhance your promotability traits.

Response:

Q: What is critical thinking? relationship and how it can enhance your promotability traits.

Response:

Q: Tell me in your own words how asking questions supports critical thinking?

Response:

Q: Have you ever analyzed the type of questions you ask?

Response:

Q: What did you find when you researched three questioning resources? Let's discuss.

Response:

Q: How will you know you are improving your questioning ability?

Response:

Q: How can you help your team members become better at asking questions rather than jumping to conclusions or voicing their opinions?

Response:

Q: Compare and contrast two people on your team and their critical thinking ability.

Response:

Q: Create a plan for continuing to develop your critical thinking skills.

Response:

Q: How can I support you in the area of questioning?

Response:

R

RESPONSIBILITY

" You cannot escape the
responsibility of tomorrow
by evading it today.

— Abraham Lincoln

Self-Assessment Questions

Question:

What does the above quote mean to you?

Response:

Question:

Be prepared to talk to your boss at your next coaching meeting.

Response:

Question:

What additional project would you like to take on and discuss with your boss?

Response:

Question:

What skills and knowledge do you want to develop next?

Response:

Question:

Do you see opportunities to help a team member who may be overworked? What are they? Be ready to discuss.

Response:

Question:

In what area do you want to become an expert?

Response:

Question:

Taking the initiative is critical to the promotion pathway. If you took a self-assessment, would you consider yourself average or a high-potential employee? What initiative have you taken or could seek to change the situation?

Response:

Coach/Mentor Questions

Q: *You cannot escape the responsibility of tomorrow by evading it today.*
— Abraham Lincoln. What does this quote mean to you?

Response:

Q: Let's discuss you taking on more responsibility at work. What additional project would you like to take on?

Response:

Q: What skills and knowledge do you want to develop next?

Response:

Q: What do you think senior managers value in high-potential employees?

Response:

Q: Do you see opportunities to help a team member who may be overworked?

Response:

Q: In what area do you want to become an expert?

Response:

Q: Have you set up a daily Google© alert to get started? On what topic(s)?

Response:

Q: How can you develop taking the initiative?

Response:

Q: How can I support you in the area of responsibility?

Response:

S

SELF-AWARENESS

" Knowing yourself is key to
all wisdom.

— Aristotle

Self-Assessment Questions

Question:

Based on the interviews you conducted what did you learn?

Response:

Question:

What are three of your strength areas?

Response:

Question:

What are two areas that need to be developed?

Response:

Question:

What is one thing they find frustrating about you?

Response:

Question:

What do they wish for you?

Response:

Question:

What is an area of expertise for you?

Response:

Question:

What are your blind spots?

Response:

Question:

How can you improve and challenge yourself?

Response:

Coach/Mentor Questions

Q: Based on the interviews you conducted what did you learn?

Response:

Q: Based on the interviews you conducted what surprised you?

Response:

Q: Have you taken any online self-awareness assessments? If yes, what did you learn or confirm?

Response:

Q: Have you ever taken any personal-development courses to discover your blind spots? If so, what courses? What did you find out?

Response:

Q: To be considered a high-potential candidate, what traits are essential to leadership or promotability?

Response:

Q: How can I support you in your quest for self-assessment?

Response:

T

THANK YOU

"Make it a habit of telling people thank you. To express your appreciation, sincerely and without the expectation of anything in return. Truly appreciate those around you, and you'll soon find many others around you. Truly appreciate life, and honestly you will find you have more of it.

— Ralph Marston

Self-Assessment Questions

Question:

Where have you noticed opportunities to say thank you?

Response:

Question:

Have you noticed missed opportunities to say thank you?

Response:

Question:

How does it make you feel when you say or write a thank you note?

Response:

Question:

Does this come naturally?

Response:

Question:

Do you need to schedule a reminder on your calendar?

Response:

Question:

How important in business do you think it is to say thank you?

Response:

Coach/Mentor Questions

Q: There is a statement that is often quoted that "employees do not quit organizations, they quit people." What does this mean to you?

Response:

Q: What kind of employee or leader do you want to be?

Response:

Q: How important is it that employees and team members feel appreciated?

Response:

Q: What makes you feel appreciated at work?

Response:

Q: Where have you noticed opportunities to say thank you?

Response:

Q: Have you noticed missed opportunities to say thank you?

Response:

Q: How important in business do you think it is to say thank you?

Response:

Q: How can I further support you in developing your "thank-you" muscle?

Response:

U

UNIQUE

" A human being is a single being. Unique and unrepeatable.
— Eileen Caddy

Self-Assessment Questions

Question:

Where are you exceptional?

Response:

Question:

What do you love doing?

Response:

Question:

What do you enjoy?

Response:

Question:

How can you serve others?

Response:

Question:

What inspires you?

Response:

Coach/Mentor Questions

Q: Each and every person is unique. Where are you exceptional? How does that serve you?

Response:

Q: What do you love doing?

Response:

Q: Who does it serve?

Response:

Q: How can you share this with others?

Response:

Q: What do you enjoy? How can you share with others to better serve them?

Response:

Q: What inspires you? How can you use your inspiration to serve others?

Response:

Q: What have you always wanted to do? How can that serve others?

Response:

VISION

The visionary starts with
a clean sheet of paper
and reimagines the world.
— Malcolm Gladwell

Self-Assessment Questions

Question:

What do you want for yourself and your life?

Response:

Question:

What type of career? What job roles? What salary do you want to earn?

Response:

Question:

What do you want for financial security?

Response:

Question:

What educational level do you want to attain?

Response:

Question:

Where do you want to live?

Response:

Question:

What do you want your relationships to look like?

Response:

Question:

What hobbies do you enjoy?

Response:

Question:

What about spirituality?

Response:

Who do you see yourself becoming? How does it feel? What do you see? Write it down. Create a vision board. Create a board that inspires you, motivates, and brings you joy. Place it some place where you see it every day.

Response:

Coach/Mentor Questions

Q: As an emerging leader, it is imperative that you have a vision of where you want to take the organization, or department or team. How would you describe the picture?

Response:

Q: What is the story?

Response:

Q: If you were the leader, could you lead the picnic exercise as described? How would you bring in all the senses? Share your version of this exercise with me.

Response:

W

WHITE LIES

" White lies always introduce others of a darker complexion.

— William S. Paley

Self-Assessment Questions

Question:

Where have you told white lies?

Response:

Question:

How did you justify it?

Response:

Question:

What did it cost you? Or what could it cost you?

Response:

Question:

Do you ever think white lies become more significant over time?

Response:

Coach/Mentor Questions

Q: What did you think about "Amnesty Day" and the returned pens?

Response:

Q: Do you think most people feel justified in telling white lies? What do you think the point of it is?

Response:

Q: Do you think there is ever a time when a white lie is justified?

Response:

Q: As a future leader, how can you create a culture of truth and integrity?

Response:

Q: How do you model transparency?

Response:

Q: How can I support you?

Response:

X-FACTOR

"
The X-Factor saved me.

— James Arthur

Self-Assessment Questions

Question:

What is your X Factor?

Response:

Question:

What is your unique talent?

Response:

Question:

How can you positively impact the outcome of the organization in your role?

Response:

Question:

Can you relate to any of the seven exceptional leadership traits?

Response:

a. Authentic

b. Depth

c. Eclectic

d. Energy of Being

e. Generosity of Spirit

f. Texture

g. Visionary

Question:

How many of these talents do you possess?

Response:

Question:

Given your assessment, would you want to promote you?

Response:

Coach/Mentor Questions

Q: Let's discuss each of these seven traits of an exceptional leader. What does it mean to be Authentic?

Response:

Q: What does it mean to have Depth?

Response:

Q: What does it mean to be Eclectic? What experiences do you bring?

Response:

Q: What is your Energy level? How resilient are you in bad times? Give me an example.

Response:

Q: Do you feel you have a Generosity of Spirit? Do you think you have the ability to connect and relate to human beings?

Response:

Q: Do you have Texture? Do you have the ability to bring a sense of creativity when approaching each situation? Give me an example.

Response:

Q: Do you feel that one day you have the ability to be Visionary? Do you think you have the ability to inspire others to achieve the vision, mission, and goals? Give me an example.

Response:

Q: How can I support you?

Response:

Y

YEARNING

" There are three ingredients for a good life: learning, earning, and yearning.

— Christopher Morley

Self-Assessment Questions

Question:

What do you yearn for?

Response:

Question:

Where do you start to make this happen?

Response:

Question:

What could stop you?

Response:

Question:

What is your timeline?

Response:

Question:

How will you measure success?

Response:

Coach/Mentor Questions

Q: What do you yearn for?

Response:

Q: Where do you start to make this happen?

Response:

Q: What could stop you?

Response:

Q: What is your timeline?

Response:

Q: How will you measure success?

Response:

Q: How can I support you?

Response:

Z

ZONE

" Everything is energy, and that's all there is to it. Match the frequency of the reality you want, and you can't help but get that reality. It can be no other way. This is not philosophy. This is physics.

— Albert Einstein

Self-Assessment Questions

Question:

Are you in the zone?

Response:

Question:

Describe when you were in the zone and how it felt.

Response:

Question:

Do you feel you are in the zone now?

Response:

Question:

How can you get back in the zone?

Response:

Question:

Read the article by Sarah Chang and check out the resources.

Response:

Question:

Final Reflection: Write our what you believe you have accomplished over the last 26 weeks. Be ready to discuss.

Response:

Question:

What is next?

Response:

Coach/Mentor Questions

Q: Are you in the zone?

Response:

Q: After reading the article by Sarah Chang what do you think?

Response:

Q: How can you help your team get in the zone?

Response:

Q: How can I support you?

Response:

Q: Final Reflection: Now that you have completed 26 weeks, what do you believe you have accomplished? Use the self-awareness inventory again to evaluate your progress.

Response:

Q: What have you learned?

Response:

Q: How have you changed?

Response:

Q: What is next?

Response:

Self-Assessment Inventory

Now that you have completed the 26 weeks, take the inventory again and explain how you have changed.

ABC's of Promotability	Plan to Improve/Resources Utilized
Rate Yourself 1-10. 1 Being Poor, 10 Being Excellent.	
1 2 3 4 5 6 7 8 9 10 Attitude	
1 2 3 4 5 6 7 8 9 10 Brand	
1 2 3 4 5 6 7 8 9 10 Communication	
1 2 3 4 5 6 7 8 9 10 Depth	
1 2 3 4 5 6 7 8 9 10 Energy	
1 2 3 4 5 6 7 8 9 10 Focus	
1 2 3 4 5 6 7 8 9 10 Gratitude	

ABC's of Promotability	Plan to Improve/Resources Utilized
Rate Yourself 1-10. 1 Being Poor, 10 Being Excellent.	
1 2 3 4 5 6 7 8 9 10 Habits	
1 2 3 4 5 6 7 8 9 10 Integrity	
1 2 3 4 5 6 7 8 9 10 Jaded	
1 2 3 4 5 6 7 8 9 10 Knowledgeable	
1 2 3 4 5 6 7 8 9 10 Life-Long Learner	
1 2 3 4 5 6 7 8 9 10 Mindset	
1 2 3 4 5 6 7 8 9 10 Network	
1 2 3 4 5 6 7 8 9 10 Opportunity	
1 2 3 4 5 6 7 8 9 10 Problem-Solver	
1 2 3 4 5 6 7 8 9 10 Question	

ABC's of Promotability	Plan to Improve/Resources Utilized
Rate Yourself 1-10. 1 Being Poor, 10 Being Excellent.	

1	2	3	4	5	6	7	8	9	10

Responsibility

1	2	3	4	5	6	7	8	9	10

Self-Awareness

1	2	3	4	5	6	7	8	9	10

Thank You

1	2	3	4	5	6	7	8	9	10

Unique

1	2	3	4	5	6	7	8	9	10

Vision

1	2	3	4	5	6	7	8	9	10

White Lies

1	2	3	4	5	6	7	8	9	10

X-Factor

1	2	3	4	5	6	7	8	9	10

Yearning

1	2	3	4	5	6	7	8	9	10

Zone

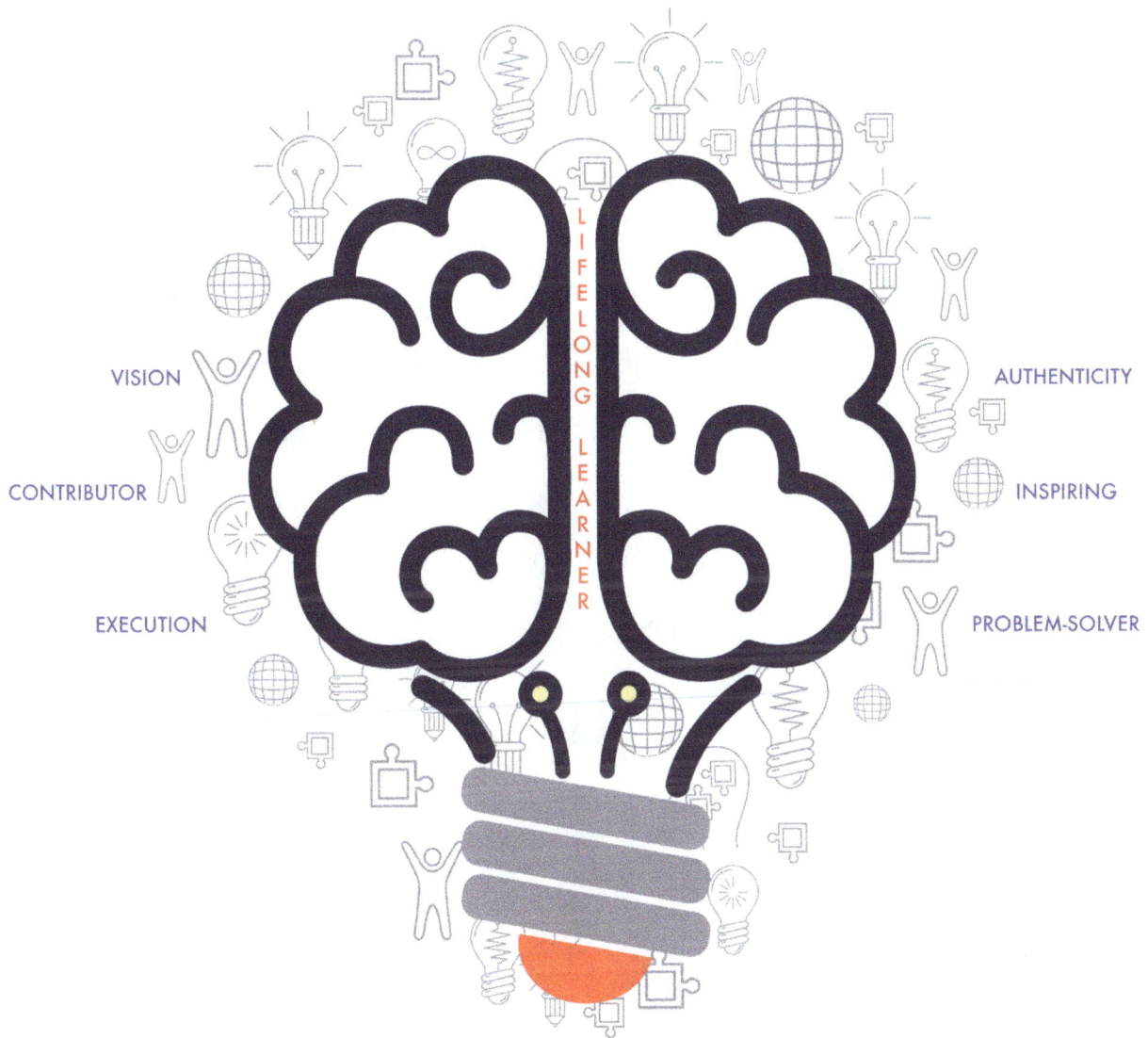

VISION

CONTRIBUTOR

EXECUTION

LIFELONG LEARNER

AUTHENTICITY

INSPIRING

PROBLEM-SOLVER

PROMOTION PROTOCOL™

www.PromotionProtocol.com

PROMOTION PROTOCOL™

COACHING CONVERSATIONS

Become Visible. Own Your Power. Get Promoted.

This book, Coaching Conversations, will allow you to:

- Personalize your learning journey for the proven pathway to promotability.

- Create engaging experiences that ignite your passion.

- Innovatively coach others to become your legacy.

- Collaboratively inspire others through artful communication.

Promotion Protocol Coaching Conversations provides a coaching framework and personalized space that allows the supervisor and the employee to collaborate and unlock the secrets of promotability and career success. The process capitalizes on the experience of the supervisor or the coach and includes the uniqueness of a new generation through weekly coaching meetings over 26 weeks. This book is a companion guide to the #1 bestseller book, "Promotion Protocol," by award-winning author, Dr. Kim Nugent.

Get Connected:

www.PromotionProtocol.com

ISBN 978-1-62747-282-1

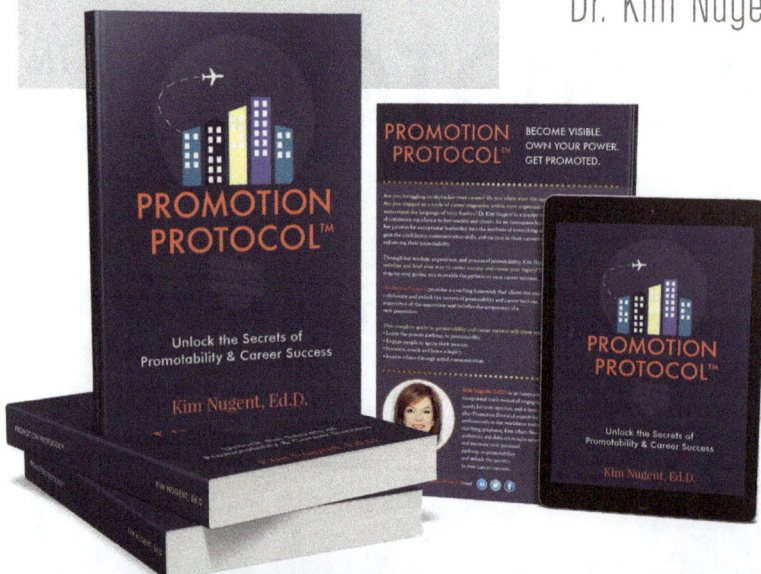

www.ingramcontent.com/pod-product-compliance
Lightning Source LLC
Chambersburg PA
CBHW081105220326

41598CB00038B/7237